Table of Contents

Introduction

The use of Art therapy is rising to popularity. Time and again it has proved to be an effective psychotherapy for victims of various mental issues. It has created a smooth platform for therapists and patients to communicate in a whole different way.

Art therapy and other forms of Expressive therapy have created a new alternative approach to medicine, achieving positive responses from people who grapple with mental health issues such as severe anxiety, stress, dementia, depression, and much besides.

These days, people are progressively falling back on art therapy to alleviate stress, reduce physical and emotional pain, heal depression, overcome a traumatic event, regain memory, develop oneself, and much more. The confirmed benefits of this practice have given hope to those who can't get the help they need from standard therapy.

This book dissects every aspect of Art and Expressive Therapy, defines them, and extensively explains the benefits. Furthermore, it will address the various forms of Expressive Therapy: drawing therapy, color therapy, clay therapy; drama therapy, dance/movement therapy, music therapy, and writing therapy. Moreover, this eBook will explore the brain structure and its functions under the heading of Neuroscience and Art Therapy.

This eBook is a reservoir of intrinsic information that could help you deal with various mental health challenges while sowing the seeds to happiness.

What is Art Therapy?

There is an artist born with almost every human being on earth. And art therapy is the method through which that artist can be awoken and brought to an active state of life. Art therapy is a therapeutic treatment established on the theories of psychotherapy but it's the kind that utilizes art and creativity to have a better interaction with patients and treat them accordingly.

Art therapy is defined in various forms by various professionals and organizations. The American Art Therapy Association briefs this treatment as

"a form of psychotherapy that uses art media as its primary mode of communication. Clients who can use art therapy may have a wide range of difficulties, disabilities or diagnoses. These include, for example, emotional, behavioral or mental health problems, learning or physical disabilities, life-limiting conditions, brain-injury or neurological conditions and physical illness. It is not a recreational activity or an art lesson, although the sessions can be enjoyable."

The British Association of Art Therapist says that

"Art therapy is a mental health profession that uses the creative process of art making to improve and enhance the physical, mental and emotional well-being of individuals

of all ages. It is based on the belief that the creative process involved in artistic self-expression helps people to resolve conflicts and problems, develop interpersonal skills, manage behavior, reduce stress, increase self-esteem and self-awareness, and achieve insight. Art therapy integrates the fields of human development, visual art (drawing, painting, sculpture, and other art forms), and the creative process with models of counseling and psychotherapy"

And the International Art Therapy Organization classifies it in tow sections:

1. *"Art therapy is the idea that the process of making art is therapeutic; this process is sometimes referred to as art as therapy. Art making is seen as an opportunity to express oneself imaginatively, authentically, and spontaneously, an experience that, over time, can lead to personal fulfillment, emotional reparation, and transformation."*

2. *"Arttherapy is based on the idea that art is a means of symbolic communication. This approach, often referred to as art psychotherapy, emphasizes the products--drawings, paintings, and other art expressions--as helpful in communicating issues, emotions, and conflicts."*

Professionals use different terminologies to describe this practice, but their goal is more or less the same and that is to extract the healing power of art and remedy the various threats to human life. It is used to treat stress, depression, chronic illness, memory loss, even post-traumatic stress disorder (PTSD).

Art therapists have to scrutinize artworks to diagnose, treat or understand a patient's mental condition. Art is the produce of the mind's labor. So on a canvas, paper, or any creative work, the artist's mindset can be read. And an art therapist has to analyze every segment of that art piece to voice a professional opinion and come to a conclusion. So they are trained and certified professionals in both fields of art and therapy.

Art therapy can be conducted in both clinical and non-clinical settings such as art studios and work-shops. But as stated earlier the therapist has to be a certified professional. The setting of an art therapy session does not resemble traditional art classes. As the author of 'The Art Therapy Sourcebook' Cathy Maldioch explains it

"In most art therapy sessions, the focus is on your inner experience – your feelings, perceptions, and imagination. While art therapy may involve learning skills or art techniques, the emphasis is generally first on developing and expressing images that come from inside the person, rather than those he or she sees in the outside world."

What differentiates art therapy from other kinds of creative art therapies is that it does not require the application of words or movement. Communication in art therapy is conducted through the various mediums of visual art, such as painting drawing, photography, digital art, and sculpting.

Art therapy is a fairly young therapeutic medium. The practice of this profession just began in the mid-20th century by Adrian Hill, a British artist and author of the book 'Art Versus Illness.'

"Releasing the creative energy of the frequently inhibited patient will build up a strong defense against the misfortunes of life,"

Hill noted.

The first organization ever established for Art Therapy was the British Association of Art Therapists in 1964. Then in 1969 the establishment of the American Art Therapy Association followed.

The practice is currently being recognized and institutionalized in many countries around the globe; Sweden, Japan, Canada, Brazil, Finland and so forth.

Who can benefit from Art Therapy
The best thing about Art Therapy is that it doesn't ask for you to have the mad skills of Leonardo da Vinci or Picasso to be admitted and reap its benefits. Also, it doesn't have age limits. So it's basically meant for me, you, him, her – Everyone!

Children

Art therapy is incredibly beneficial for children, especially for those who are challenging the misfortunes of life brought on by a disability or mental health problems. In such circumstances verbal expression can be extraordinarily difficult for them. And that is where art therapy comes in handy.

This treatment paves the way for these children to fluently communicate their thoughts, needs and emotions to their therapist and guardians.

When dealing with children, art therapists use a method that is quite different from the kind they use on adult patients. They first provide the child with age-appropriate art materials then ask for them to express themselves in whatever kind of drawing or painting.

The therapist would then analyze the completed work then ask the child about certain elements of the art piece; what it is meant to symbolize, depict and so forth. Taking note of the answers, the therapist would then have the comprehensive knowledge of the problem and craft a treatment program that would effectively work for the infant.

Art therapy is known to be most effective in helping children cope or recover from learning disabilities, mental health disorder such as schizophrenia or depression, stress, trauma caused by mental, physical or sexual abuse. It can even help children understand and deal with physical disabilities.

Adults

Adulthood is the time in which the activities in life reach their peak. And we all know how life and its endless stream of chaotic events can take an emotional toll on anyone. So, most adults are highly susceptible to stress, depression, confusion, and low self-esteem. And when there is injury, a haunting past, or loss of a loved added to this uneasy lifestyle, the emotional turmoil can be taken to a different level.

For those adults who are emotionally ensnared in such debacles and find difficulties in expressing themselves verbally, art therapy is basically a one way ticket to recovery.

Stress

Who lives a life free of stress in the 21st century? With a pile of bills demanding your urgent attention, with work, deadlines, friends, family, and so much more to worry about, how could you not end up with a throbbing headache? Even the rich and famous have a thing or two to worry about. So yes it's normal to be stressful.

Some studies even show the benefits of stress. It is said that the physical changes brought on by stress increase ones strength and stamina, speed up reaction time and enhance focus abilities.

But here's the thing, stress has a rippling effect, the kind to jeopardize ones overall health if it is without limits.

Experts in the medical field have confirmed its role in creating problems such as acne, headache, depression, anxiety, asthma, heart disease, high blood pressure and much besides.

A lot of people suffer from acute stress. And for relief, most of them resort to substances such as alcohol, tobacco and drugs which are more harmful to them than useful. Art therapy, though, offers those who are suffering from severe stress a sustainable remedy.

The activities in art therapy don't only distract the patient from negative thoughts but also help him/her meditate upon oneself. At first this will lead to the reduction of stress but then the patient will be able to get to the core of what is causing the stress and get rid of it once and for all.

Depression

A lot of people suffer from depression. It is a common disease amongst society. And its causes range from a traumatic event, injury, illness, to a haunting past.

Depression is the kind of illness that leaves a person emotionally drained,feeling hopeless, confused and futile. The fatalistic views of life depression creates is very difficult to overcome. And when its leftuntreated it can lead up to extreme exhaustion, insomnia, eating disorder and much besides.

Aside from the physical side effects, depression can destroy relationships, one's social life, job performance, and so much more. Studies have also shown that people suffering from depression are more susceptible to heart related diseases.

Art therapy can be an effective remedy for such severe conditions.

Verbal expression can at times be a struggle for those suffering from depression. But through art - painting, drawing, or sculpting- they can unravel the true identity of their problems and depict them with the uttermost ease.

Art therapy facilitates the communication between a patient and his/her emotions. It paves the way to self-discovery, self-respect, and happiness.

Note: Most depressants are composed to stimulate the release of the chemical neurotransmitter dopamine— the pleasure center of the brain. According to recent studies, similar chemicals are released when we look at art.

Veterans

Art therapy is known to be most effective on veterans who return home with a certain kind of psychological or medical disorder.

After the winter VA Hospital began providing art therapy as a component of their psychiatric services to veterans returning from WWII, it became an indispensable element in almost all veterans' hospitals offering mental health services.

Post-traumatic Stress Disorder (PTSSD) has gravely affected veterans since World War I, and when art therapy was applied as a treatment for this chronic condition, positive results have shown.

Through art-based relaxation techniques and coping skills, a veteran's cognitive skill is sustained and stress is reduced to a great degree. Art therapy enables a veteran to express and resolve daunting memories of traumatic events; it promotes positive thinking, self-worth and self-esteem.

For veterans with physical injuries, art therapy helps them understand and accept the physical changes and injuries they have undergone. It encourages them to have a positive outlook of their condition and help them find the strength to recover and live a full and happy life.

Neuroscience and Art Therapy

The human brain remains a very intricate entity but cutting-edge discoveries have helped demystify it. Since time immemorial, the brain was viewed as an unchangeable structure; however, probing researches done in neuroscience have revealed fascinating facts about this vital organ.

Contrary to the long established belief and according to the neuroscience investigations, the brain happens to be an organ that can physically grow, change and revitalize. This capacity of the brain is known as *neuroplasticity*. Human experiences, thoughts and actions can indeed mold the brain.

Neuroplasticity, experts claim, is the keystone in the comprehension of the connection between neuroscience and art therapy. Images conjured up by the imagination have the potential of producing neurotransmitters and hormones, of restructuring the human brain and much besides. Focusing on selected images through the art-making process and visual expression can enhance intellectual capacity, social relations and physical healing.

The Brain Structure and its Functions

As the author Diane Akeman tellingly phrases it:

> *"We take for granted . . . the undeniable fact that each person carries around atop the body a complete universe in which trillions . . . of sensations, thoughts and desires stream.... Our brain is a crowded chemistry lab, bustling with nonstop neuro conversations."*

So that's for metaphors, but it does well to depict the profound complexity of the brain –a complexity that is far beyond the gamut of this book to discuss. So let's keep it simple. Structurally the brain can be divided into various sectors such as lobes, cortices and hemispheres. Here, the various regions are conveniently dissected for better understanding of its functions.

Cerebrum

The cerebrum, otherwise known as the neocortex, is a distinctive part of the brain that distinguishes humans from animals. It permits oral language functions and intricate cognition. It consists of the frontal lobe, parietal lobe, temporal lobe, and occipital lobe. The neocortex with its lobes encases the limbic system (which will be discussed later).

I. The Frontal Lobe

As suggested by the name, this is the lobe located at the anterior. It is seen as the thinking part of the brain. The frontal part of this lobe—the prefrontal cortex— carries out the cognitive functions such as: personality and behavior, intellect, problem solving, the process of abstract thought, creative thought, attention, inhibition, certain emotion, and reasoning.

The rear of the frontal lobe, the motor cortex and pre-motor cortex, control: movement coordination, muscle movements, comprehensive and mass movements, certain eye movements, skilled movements, sense of smell, physical reaction etc.

II. The Parietal Lobe

This area is receptive to the sensations of touch, temperature, pain and pressure. It is also associated with language and body scheme. Among its functions are:

tactile sensation (sense of touch), proprioception (reaction to interior stimulation), sensory comprehension and combination, some visual functions and certain functions of reading and language.

Reading disabilities stem from dysfunctions of the lower section of the parietal lobe.

III. The Temporal Lobe

This lobe has two sections that carry out different functions. The upper part takes on the auditory role and the lower part deals with memory. This region is responsible for some behavior and emotions, sense of identity, certain hearing, music, fear, some vision pathways, visual memories, auditory memories, certain language and speech functions.

Damage inflicted on the temporal lobe can result in the inability to comprehend language (receptive aphasia) and impair hearing and memory functions.

IV. The Occipital lobe

Found at the rear and lowest section of the neocortex, this lobe is the focal point of the visual process as it is directly connected to the eyes through the optic nerves. It is thus primarily responsible for vision.

Injury to this region could result in vision impairment or blindness.

The Limbic System

Located closely to the interior walls of each cerebral hemisphere, this system of brain nuclei is believed to be the seat of primitive emotions like sadness, fear, anger, happiness, aggression and revulsion. It also has a role in establishing recent memories. Its functions are carried out through extensive neural connections linked to the neocortex and the brain stem.

The Brain Stem

This is the lower region of the brain that receives stimuli from the sensory receptors. It serves as a filtering agent that decides whether the various electro-chemical discharges (impulses) sent to it through the spinal tract should be prohibited or put through the intricate neural processing.

Furthermore, the brain stem is a key player in the intrinsic functions of breathing, swallowing, blood pressure, heart rate, arousal of various kinds and consciousness.

The Right Hemisphere and Left Hemisphere

Interestingly, the right hemisphere manages maintains the left parts of the body while the left hemisphere manages the right parts of the body. Therefore, damage inflicted on the left hemisphere of the brain impairs movement on the right side and vice versa.

The left hemisphere deals with the logical and sequential process. It produces and understands language. It is the right hemisphere that handles temporal and spatial relationships, analyzes nonverbal information, expresses and recognizes emotions.

Art Therapy in Concert with Neuroscience

Advances made in neuroscience allow for a better understanding of the brain and help pave the way for various avenues to apply art therapy.

Art therapy mainly helps in the rebuilding and treatment of physical injury, the enhancement of emotional, mental and physical therapy and the promotion of emotional and cognitive growth.

Kinesthetic and Sensory Stimulation

This is the combination of sensory-tactile, kinesthetic-motor and contact with the art media that in tandem induce essential motor movement. Kinesthetic action can be especially useful in the treatment of patients with Alzheimer's disease, chronic schizophrenics, and stroke victims. The stimulation of the touch sensory can go round damaged regions of the brain and restore memories.

Tactile interaction with art media such as paste, finger paints and clay promotes new development for children and adults who are developmentally impaired. It can also stimulate emotional reactions.

Visual Synopsis

A lot can be assessed from the drawing of patients. In dealing with victims of Alzheimer's disease, art therapists study the art work of their patients to discover their unconscious and conscious behavior imprinted in their drawings.

According to the findings of Menzen, K. H. (2001), those injured in the right hemisphere lack the ability to perceive and depict a whole picture in their drawings; where as those with impairments on the left hemisphere produce artwork that can be described as repetitive and schematic. In dealing with these patients art therapy involving the building of three-dimensional structures of wood blocks and foam was applied. This was to create new neural pathways and functional reformation. Two different approaches were adopted. For those with damages on their left hemisphere, focus on details and sequences were implemented, and for individuals with injuries in the right hemisphere emphasis was put on reconstruction and spatial perception.

Expressive Therapy

Expressive therapy, otherwise known as creative arts therapy, expressive arts therapy or expressive therapies, is a kind of therapy that employs creative arts as a medium to treat patients. It is believed that imagination and creative expression has the power to heal peoples.

Expressive therapy is term that constitutes many kinds of therapeutic treatments; amongst them are:

Art therapy

A therapeutic mechanism for solving problems, growing social skills, reconciling emotional conflicts, curtailing anxiety and much besides via the medium of art, imagery and creative process.

Music Therapy

This is a form of therapy through which music is employed to develop cognitive, psychological, physical or communal functions.

Drama Therapy

In this therapeutic approach drama/theater processes, products, and associations are employed to induce emotional and physical integration, personal growth and symptom relief. This permits the individual to express his/her story to attain catharsis, solve an issue, and comprehend the meaning of images and much more.

Dance/movement therapy

It is believed that dance/movement therapy can bring changes to physical functioning, behavior, cognition and feelings.

Writing, Poetry, and Bibliotherapy

Used synonymously, Bibliotherapy and poetry therapy are deployed for the purposes of bringing personal growth and healing.

One is not required to be versed in the arts, dance, poetry, or drama to practice expressive therapy. This practice could be for anyone who desires to achieve the benefits creative arts therapy contains.

Full elaboration on the types of expressive therapy and how to practice it is on the next few chapters.

History

Nowadays, expressive therapies are employed as an alternative approach in medicine, mental health, and rehabilitation. Nevertheless, history proves that throughout the existence of mankind art has been employed as a therapeutic and healing agent since antiquity. For instance, it is reported that the Egyptians used to embolden people who suffered from mental illness to participate in artistic activity (Freshman &Fryrear, The arts in therapy, 1981); the Greeks used music and drama for its mending characteristics (Gladding 1992).

During the Renaissance, according to Robert Burton's theory (the English physician and writer), the role of the imagination was crucial in terms of well-being and health. De Feltre (the Italian philosopher), moreover, argued that playing and dancing were extremely significant to children's development and growth.

The proper use of the arts as a supplementary medical treatment came into play from the late 19th century to the 20th century.

According to Joseph Moreno (the founder of psychodrama) mental health can be reinstated through the use of enactment.

The creative art therapies became vastly popular during the 30s and 40s.During this period, artists and psychotherapists began to realize that self-expression via non-verbal ways such as movement, painting and music might be beneficial to patients with mental ailments.

Nowadays, expressive therapies are utilized as subordinate and main forms of treatment. They are applied in medical, rehabilitative and mental health settings. For instance, music and imaginary theatre are now deployed regularly for pain reduction, childbirth, and relaxation. Play and art have proved their efficacy in debriefing, resolution and trauma. Writing has been applied to improve illnesses like arthritis, asthma, and to also reduce post traumatic stress in individuals who have encountered the loss of a loved one or a traumatic event.

It's characteristic.

Expressive therapy entails specific characteristics that you usually don't find in verbal therapies:

1. Self-expression

2. Active participation

3. Imagination

4. Mind-body connections

Self-expression

Emboldening individuals to engage in self-expression is in the very nature and aim of all therapies. Expressive therapy not only stimulates self-exploration, but also utilizes self-expression through various modalities as the pivotal component of the procedures of therapy.

Most therapies use the fullest potential of music, play, art, and writing. This is because expressing oneself through movement, painting, or poetry can recap events of the past and also produce catharsis for some patients.

Active Participation

Psychology defines expressive art therapy as "action therapies" as they are action-oriented mechanisms that facilitate the sharing of feelings and thoughts, and the exploring of personal issues. A person makes bodily movements when participating in activities involving drama, dance, art, music, writing, and others.

Art making, for instance, involves preparing, painting, forming, touching, drawing, etc.

Expressive therapies prompt patients to participate actively during the process of therapy. It's believed that participants can actually be energized through the experience of creating and making.

Furthermore, it allows individuals to completely focus on issues, goals, and behaviors, while alleviating stress.

Imagination

Some prefer "creativity" to describe expressive therapy. However, it is indeed imagination that lays the foundation for practice and theory. Experimentation, self-expression, and subsequent verbal reflection are produced through imaginative thinking.

Mind-body Connection

According to the NCCAM (National Center for Complementary and Alternative Medicine) mind-body interventions are purposed to develop the capacity of the mind to influence the functions of the body and symptoms.

The inroads in neurodevelopment and neuroscience have drawn attention to the effect expressive therapies have in the mind-body interventions. Particularly, when dealing with physical illness, behavioral disorders, and stress disorders.

For instance, drama and art therapies are expected to amend posttraumatic stress and facilitate the expression of past traumatic events.

Music therapy

Music is employed during Music Therapy to encourage positive changes and help achieve individualized goals. These improved changes may be seen physically, emotionally, mentally, socially, spiritually, or aesthetically. Music therapy is employed as one of the main treatment options to curtail depression, anxiety, or other mental health issues, as it is considered to be very effective.

Our brain chemistry can change by listening to pleasant music. In a natural way, music can assist in increasing the serotonin levels, which makes a person feel good. Serotonin is a neurotransmitter which is responsible for "good moods." According to research, the benefits reaped from Music Therapy to treat depression are considerable in comparison with standard treatment. In other words, major improvements have been noticed in patients who received Music therapy.

A Brief History of Music Therapy

Music has been used in medicine since ancient times. Ancient Greek philosophers believed that music could heal both the body and the soul. Greek physician Hippocrates— widely deemed to be the father of modern medicine— utilized music as the prominent healing device for treating mental patients in the ancient Greek era.

Aristotle maintained the belief that music has the power to purify the emotions. In accord with a popular belief, Egyptians used music to alleviate pain in labor and subsequent childbirth. Moreover, Native Americans and several other indigenous peoples have employed singing and chanting as part of their healing rituals for thousands of years.

English scholar, Robert Burton, noted in his classic book 'The Anatomy of Melancholy' (first published in 1621), that music and dance were indispensable in treating mental illness, especially melancholy.

After World War I and World War II, community musicians who were both amateur and professionals, visited veteran hospitals around the country to sing for the thousands of veterans sustaining both physical and emotional trauma caused by the war. The patient's remarkable responses to the music culminated in the hiring of many musicians in medical institutions.

Who can benefit from music therapy?

Children, adolescents, adults, and elderly people with mental health ailments like Alzheimer's disease, substance abuse problems, brain injuries, physical disabilities, acute and chronic pain.

Music & Depression

Music is indeed being used as an alternative medicine for the treatment of anxiety, depression, and other health issues. The benefits of music in therapy are a great deal for mental health. Its perks could be witnessed in anxiety and stress reduction, betterment of the functional skills, and the increase of relaxation.

Music can assist in motivating a person to express him/herself. To overcome depression, one must need to acknowledge the situation and accept the condition. This happens to be one of the most crucial aspects of rising above depression. Writing songs of your own can help you better focus on your true feelings and discover what you are going through. Listening to soothing music will help you relax when you are stressed. It stimulates a calm response which can thereby culminate in psychological changes in the body. Studies have shown that people with severe depression demonstrated notable improvements in mood and found that music therapy helped them overcome their verbal barriers to expressing their emotion.

Music you can use to reduce stress:

Native American, Indian, Celtic stringed instrument, flutes, and drums are very effectual for mind relaxation. Furthermore, *sounds of thunder, rain, and sounds of nature combined with light jazz and classical* will also serve as a relaxation device.

This, not the least bit, means that you should exert yourself to listen to music that irks you. This will pose as a setback instead of making progress. If you find yourself in that position, try getting musical suggestion or contact Counseling Service.

Dementia

Among the disorders that are treated with music therapy is Alzheimer's disease and other types of dementia. Patients that suffered from dementia have proven to benefit from music therapy. Music is one of the components employed to aid recalling memories. In fact, several people, with brains that are healthy, find themselves recalling past memories when their favorite music is on. Patients who are treated for dementia often experience the same feelings. They recall events and people that are connected to their past.

Patients sustaining memory loss or lack of ability to speak often grapple with articulating what they think and therefore eschew from having a conversation with others. This unwillingness to communicate normally worsens the disease. One way dementia is treated in music therapy is by playing the patients' favorite song. During this session the patient is emboldened to sing along. Some patients, without the encouragement of anybody, even sing with the music, every so often eventuating in unrestrained talk. Music therapies for those who suffer from dementia helps them feel emotionally secure, bestowing them confidence to interact with others.

Prenatal music therapy

Music therapy is vital during pregnancy. The fetus is able to listen to their mother's singing as well as speech at just 16 weeks. Health care professionals monitor the movements of the unborn child responding to musical stimuli through an ultrasound. We could also see the baby's ability to express its needs and interests by way of its movements in the womb. At the beginning of the second trimester, the fetus is capable of hearing maternal sounds because the ear structure is fully mature.

During pregnancy, women are likely to experience high level of stress, which could be detrimental to both the baby and the mother. To alleviate anxiety, music is used to preserve a relaxed state, as stress could increase blood pressure and weaken the immune system of both the mother and baby.

According to a research conducted, music has the power to decrease pain and also the need for morphine-like pain relief.

Listening to one's favorite music during labor, helps to activate a 'reward' within the brain incrementing dopamine and endorphins, the body's own 'happy hormones' which performs as a natural pain relief.

Pregnant women can prepare by creating their own favorite playlist.

Dance/Movement Therapy

What is Dance Movement Therapy?

"The psychotherapeutic use of movement to further emotional, cognitive, physical and social integration of the individual."

That is how the "American Dance Therapy Association" (ADTA) defines Dance/Movement Therapy (DMT).

Based on the premise that the mind and body are units which are inseparable, DMT employs dance and movement to stimulate and enhance the functions of motor, intellect, and emotion. Dance therapists believe that the feelings and attitudes of an individual are affected either positively or negatively by the muscular tension and restricted movement patterns which are created by emotional and mental problems. Therefore, they believe that through the psychotherapeutic approach of dancing can liberally express their emotions and release the tension in their muscles. Through dance a person's innermost emotions like surprise, sorrow, regret, happiness, love, aggression, fear and submission can be revealed.

The therapy of Dance/movement can be utilized to aid people dealing with a range of mental and physical issues. Individuals suffering from severe anxiety disorders or stress and depression can benefit tremendously from this practice. It has the dual benefit of helping people express feelings that are hard to speak about and of inducing a vibrant mood through the release of endorphins via the physical exercise involved. DMT is also used to treat patients with autism, Alzheimer's, Parkinson's disease and much besides.

There are both physical and mental advantages to this practice. On a physical scale individuals can reap great benefits such as improved health, muscle tone and coordination. From a physiological perspective, people become invigorated and comfortable in their own skins. It helps them uncover concealed emotions like frustration, anger, and the loss of loved ones— emotions that may be too difficult to seek through verbal means. DMT aims to enhance cognitive skills, memory and inspiration.

Types of Dance/Movement Therapies
A lot of dance styles are available for DMT. They could have cultural elements like the Turkish dance, ballroom dance, foxtrot, line dancing and tango walks. One popular Dance therapy is the Authentic Movement.

Authentic Movement

Authentic Movement (AM), also named an expressive improvisational movement, is a part of expressive therapy. It is a psychotherapeutic technique in which participants are put in a relaxed, unconscious state through the implementation of imagination and fantasy. The individuals are encouraged to express their emotions through symbolic movements. This way they reveal the unconscious mind without any reservation.

During these sessions participants start off by closing their eyes and relaxing their body. Movements are made not by the stimulus of external prompts but by the internal stimulus of their body. Their movements are impulsive directed by orders from within. They respond to this stimulus through spontaneous movements such as random jerks, certain hand moves and hand gestures. This is not only limited to silent movement; individuals can also express themselves through yelling or calling out random words while moving.

In these sessions participants are encouraged to separate themselves from rational thinking and self-analysis. The only attention they are asked to give is that directed to their senses and their inner feelings. For this to proceed accordingly the practice must remain simple and strictly intuitive.

A witness will be assigned to each person. This is the individual responsible for passively observing the person's AM without making any analysis and judgment. This is known as the relationship between the mover and witness. It can be conducted in pairs or in larger groups.

How does it Work?
Dance/Movement Therapy can be conducted on a group or individual format.

The group therapies help individuals come out of their isolated shells and establish social and emotional bonds. They also benefit from the invigorating spirit gained from the interaction with others. Relational dynamics and social skills can be enhanced through this practice.

The individual sessions are conducive to an in-depth connection between the patient and the therapist. This helps assess and treat the person's ailment selectively.

Dance/Movement Therapy consists of four stages:

1. **Preparation**: It is, by definition, a warm-up stage where the mind and body are prepared for the exercise ahead. In an area with safety parameters, the participant is allowed to move liberally with the eyes shut. This is the stage where a relationship with a witness is established.

The spontaneous motion involved in this period helps the person trust and recognize his impulses. It also helps him contain or act on these impulses selectively.

2. **Incubation**: the individual acts on the verbal instructions of the leader and slips into an imaginary world illustrated by the instructor. At this point the participant loses all control and immerses in the internal environment created thus. He then makes symbolic movements to express emotions. This promotes creativity in self-expression and paves new ways of acting and thinking.

3. **Illumination**: This is the level where the individual carries out a self-reflective act to discover and deal with subconscious emotions. The participant makes the link between the symbolic movements and their meanings.

4. **Evaluation**: This is the last stage of the therapy where the developments made are verbally discussed.

How to Choose the Right Dance/Movement Therapy Course

"I went to a Christmas party in Negombo at the Cheshire Home for the disabled. While the rest of the audience watched local school children performing, I was watching the residents of the Home - and wondered how it must feel to always be on the other side of the fence, to be excluded. That's when I decided to concentrate on investigating the possibilities of dance more carefully, perhaps making a different kind of dance theatre as a form of creative

expression for people who otherwise would never have the chance to develop their artistic potential. "

Wolfgang Stange.

When scouring for the right therapist and course, you must select one that suits you best. You will have to be certain that you are in the right hands. So research, research, research! You will have to conduct an investigation of your own. Every decision you make to find the right therapist and the right course tailored to your need must be well informed. You might get referrals from your primary-care. But in general, there are dance/movement therapists who work on an independent or a team basis. ADTA (The American Dance Therapy Association) has international operations that may be available in your local area. They operate in places like Great Britain, Canada, China, Germany, Norway, Egypt, France and Russia.

The American Dance Movement Association along with the Association for Dance Movement Psychotherapy, UK (ADMP UK) helps connect qualified dance/movement therapists with clients. ADTA has standards that therapists must meet in order to be a licensed professional. The organization has an updated list of licensed dance/movement professionals on its website.

ADMA's Standards

Dance Therapy Registered (DTR): This is a designation granted to a first-time dance therapists possessing a master's degree and has finished 700 hrs of supervised internship. A therapist of this level can work as a dance therapist but not in private practices.

Academy of Dance Therapists Registered (ADTR): This is a designation for the advanced DTRs who have accomplished 3,640 hrs of administered medical work in an institution, agency, or special schools. There are other qualifications they must meet too. These professionals are competent to work in private practices.

Standard of the Association for Dance Movement Therapy UK (ADMT UK)

In Britain there are three levels of registration for dance/movement therapists. The ADMT UK has authoritative control over the courses issued. DMT students take theoretical training of various academic disciplines such as psychology, anatomy, psychotherapy, physiology, and dance/movement therapy.

1. **Basic Registration (BRDMT):** This is basically a probational qualification that is issued for those who have finished post-graduate training in DMT.

2. **Registered Status (RDMT):** This is for the BRDMT who have finished extra hours supervised practice. This is acquired two years after the therapist is registered as a BRDMT.

3. **Senior Registered Dance Movement Therapist (SRDMT):** It is a designation for those who have completed extra hours of supervise internship and have undergone personal therapy. To qualify, these individuals are also expected to submit paper fitted for publication.

At this current point British Dance movement therapists have yet to be registered on one of the formal psychotherapy organs (UKCP for instance). But DMTs work in the National Health Service (NHS), prisons, educational facilities (for children dealing with emotional and behavioral ailments), agencies, private practices and working with children and family services.

Drama Therapy

Drama therapy falls under the category of creative art therapy or expressive art therapy. It is a recreational therapeutic program that uses drama and the setting of a theatre to treat patients.

Through drama therapy, patients are made to approach their deepest emotions, daunting memories, fears, or agony indirectly, by the use of metaphors, myths or stories.

There are various forms of activities in Drama therapy. There is Role-play, Mime, Improvisation, Movement, Acting out, Speech and so forth.

Role-play happens to be amongst the main frequently used activities in drama therapy. It is when a patient plays a character in a certain situation, as in a person trapped in an elevator or a child in some unusual event.

Mime is a style in acting that doesn't permit the use of words. So when a patient is assigned to mime, he/she will have to express the scenario and the character's emotions through body language. And Improvisation is when a patient has to make up a dialogue and a scenario right there on the spot.

Drama therapy can be conducted in different settings such as schools, private workspaces, prisons, and so forth. It is often set within a group environment, but one to one sessions are also available.

Through drama therapy people are able to enhance their social skills, have a better understanding of one-self, achieve catharsis, and much besides. It is a highly recommended treatment for couples and families.

It is known to be especially effective on those who struggle to face their emotions and problems directly.

Writing Therapy

Another form of expressive therapy is writing therapy. Writing therapy uses literature to help patients externalize their thoughts and emotions. Much like other forms of expressive therapies, it is used to treat patients with emotional burdens brought on by grief, depression, chronic illness, trauma and so forth. This method is especially effective on those who struggle in expressing their thoughts verbally or in forms of images.

Not much is required to take part in this therapeutic treatment; speaking the same language as the therapist and the ability to structure thoughts and emotions in to basic sentences are all the requirements it demands. The best part about writing therapy is that it can either be conducted face-to-face with a therapist or from a distance via email. The latter is most suited for those who prefer anonymity.

There are various styles of writing to choose from in writing therapy. There is journal writing, expressive writing, poetry writing and letter writing.

Journal writing
Journal writing, otherwise known as journal therapy, doesn't resemble the writing style used in diaries or personal journals. It is where the patient is asked to write a description of his/her emotions, reaction, and perspective of certain events in life; not the events themselves.

Through journal writing, patients are able to give their undivided attention to their emotions. And that gives way for them to analyze and have a full understanding of what is troubling their mindset.

"Through the acts of journal writing, the writer is able to literally read his/her own mind," the founder and director of The Center for Journal Therapy, quoted.

Journal writing is incredibly constructive for those suffering from insomnia. Writing about the thoughts and emotions that is obstructing them from obtaining a restful mind helps them get to the bottom of the problem and finally put an end to it.

According to the extensive research conducted by Dr. James W.Pennebaker, writing is as beneficial to the body as it is to the mind.

"The development of a coherent narrative helps to recognize ad structure traumatic memories, resulting in more adaptive internal schemas."

He explained.

Letter Writing

This is a method in which therapists ask their patients to write a letter to an individual who might either be dead or alive. You can even write a letter to yourself. The letter will not be sent but it will be followed by an imaginative response from that recipient.

It has an impeccable effect on patients who have a thing or two that were left unsaid.

Expressive Writing

Expressive writing is much like journal writing. When assigned to expressive writing, patients have to give a detailed account of some traumatic event they have gone through at some point in life, and then write about how they felt when it happened. The writing products of this style are usually very personal, deep, insightful and emotional.

At first, expressive writing is noted to take an immediate toll on patients, their stress level increases, they delve into a negative state of mind, some even experience physical pain. But once that phase comes to an end, its long-term benefits begin to unravel. Notable reductions in stress, anxiety, and depression are but a few.

Below is a sample of a writing instruction structured by Dr. James W. Pennebaker:

"Over the next four days, I want you to write about your deepest emotions and thoughts about the most upsetting experience in your life. Really let go and explore your feelings and thoughts about it. In your writing, you might tie this experience to your childhood, your relationship with your parents, people you have loved or love now, or even your career. How is this experience related to who you would like to become, who you have been in the past, or who you are

now?

Many people have not had a single traumatic experience but all of us have had major conflicts or stressors in our lives and you can write about them as well. You can write about the same issue every day or a series of different issues. Whatever you choose to write about, however, it is critical that you really let go and explore your very deepest emotions and thoughts."

Poetry writing

Poetry writing or poetry therapy is the use of written or spoken poetry for psychological treatments.

During poetry writing sessions, therapists select a stimulating poem that can encourage discussion and inspire patients to write a poem of their own.

The stimulating nature of poetry combined with the techniques of psychology creates an environment that helps patients express their thought and emotion openly and with the uttermost honesty.

Self-awareness, healthy self-esteem, enhanced communication skills, increased coping skills, creativity, stress reduction are just some of the benefits a patient can reap from poetry therapy.

Writing therapy is a method through which people can be completely honest with themselves. If the patient chooses to keep the writing products private, he/she has the option of destroying it by ways of burning, shredding and so forth.

For those who wish to make use of writing therapy without a therapist or a counselor, here is a sample guideline.

- Find the time and area that would be devoid of disturbances. A perfect timing would be when you finish work or before bedtime.
- Make a pledge to yourself to write for at least fifteen-minutes a day for three to four days consecutively.
- Continuously write, once you've started. Don't stop to bother about grammar or spelling. If you have addressed everything you wanted to write and run out of things to note down, repeat what you've wrote.
- It is totally up to you on whether you want to write longhand or use a computer to type. You can also use a tape recorder to talk if you are unable to write.
- In those three to four days, you can jot down the same things (if you want), or you can simply write about different things each day.
-

Drawing Therapy
Drawing therapy is one of the forms of expressive art therapy which involves demonstrating ones feelings,

thought, pain, stress, wishes and much besides through drawing. More often than not, many people who experienced traumatic events in their life find it problematic to talk about the details of what they remember; nevertheless drawing therapy creates a perfect and deeper outlet for self-expression.

Anyone can reap the benefits of drawing therapy. For example, drawing could be extremely useful to children, or simply those who do not feel confident or fully comfortable conveying their thoughts through just verbal means of communication. Young children usually lack the ability to articulate everything they want to say, and this could be a very exhausting journey for them. That's why most children consider drawing a safe and liberating activity. Traumatized children are more willing to express complex emotions and memories by way of drawing.

Art is an indispensible factor in surmounting mental exhaustion. It is amazing in its healing power for people who are enduring events which are traumatic and struggle to express what they feel verbally. The calming and therapeutic qualities of drawing allow you to reflect on the art that was created to help you deal with the trauma and stress. This will eventuate in total betterment in your personality and life.

Drawing is a great way for confronting your greatest fears and weaknesses in a positive way, for it will be the first stride to overcoming them. Furthermore, it will assist in finding a resolution to your inner conflicts, building self-esteem, and improving behavior.

Globally celebrated artists such as Vincent Van Gogh and Frieda Kahlo employed their work of art to overcome depressing events.

Social Benefits

Socially challenged or rather shy people are not very fond, or, in other words, frightened of going out in the public. This is because they are convinced they are the only ones suffering from a situation. It is highly recommended, for such people, to join a group therapy session so it could help the isolation feeling recede. Moreover, interacting with other people with more or less the same issues will help in breaking the self-imposed sequestered shell. Confidence will slowly but surely rise providing a platform to depict oneself through drawing as well as other types of expressive arts.

Art Therapy Exercises

Before starting on a drawing, you need to first understand that you are not required to somehow have the skills in this area. Art does not shed a single meaning of what one is willing to express, whether it's professionally made or not. It's all about releasing your emotions, feeling secure, accepting, and embracing what life has to present. Bellow is an inspiring drawing exercise for you to do until you fully venture in to it.

- Draw or paint what you're feeling. Choose a color you feel would best defines your emotion: sad?

Disappointed? Trapped? Stressed? Angry? ….
Express what you feel in your drawing in your own
way; be free and permit yourself to judge yourself.

- Only use colors that calm and make you happy.
- Draw outside. It is a fun way to relax your mind and
  integrate with nature.
- Draw your fear. Everyone is frightened of
  something, and this drawing will give you a chance
  to face it.
- Paint something you have lost in life. It could be
  someone or something you love.
- Draw images of your good traits. You will have a
  positive self-view.
- Draw yourself as a tree. Let the roots describe the
  good qualities and your strength, while the leaves
  could be the thing you want to change.
- Draw something you consider good in your life.
  Everyone has at least one thing in life they consider
  good, so think about what truly makes you happy
  and draw it.
- Draw yourself as an animal. Choose an animal you
  love or are interested in and draw it.
- Paint a rock. You could paint the rock with things
  that give you strength or the difficult things you've
  overcame in your life. This project is meant to
  empower you.

Coloring

One amazing way to express oneself is through Coloring. Colors affect our emotions, modify moods, and evaluate your inner health. Every person has their own choices of favorite colors and shades, but there are many universal colors

Color therapy is not just something for a therapist to use to analyze your condition, and to help you figure out your issues; it can be of paramount importance to treating depression. Surrounding yourself with colors that reflect tranquility, happiness, life, and energy will transfigure your thoughts to a more positive one.

It's common for people with depression to opt for a dimmer environment, wear clothes with a faded appearance, and not take out time to enjoy life.

You can affect your mood by brightening your environment and taking out time to wear brighter apparel. Even though it cannot heal your depression overall, color would be one of the fundamental factors to reducing the severity of your condition.

Don't force yourself to feel the emotions of colors, just embrace it naturally. If you find this difficult to do, consult your therapist about what impact he/she believes colors play in your life, and how you could implement them in your daily life for an effective outcome.

How can children benefit from color therapy?

Colors help children who are suffering learning disabilities, emotional disorder, and autism. Children who are angry and depressed are often given rainbow colors of Orange, Red, Green, Yellow, Blue, Violet, and Indigo as their inspiring and healing muse. They use it effectively to express how they feel.

Clay Therapy

Clay therapy is a very effective practice that helps people with various psychological ailments express their thoughts. Emotions like anger, fear, guilt, and grief that are difficult to depict in words can be easily described through this therapy.

The practice is especially effective when dealing with children and adults who contend with expressing their emotions.

Clay helps arouse bottled-up emotions and permits a person to depict thoughts and experiences that have remained buried for far too long. Through its ability to quickly absorb and represent emotions, this medium helps individuals find answers to their problems. They often uncover the origins of their anger, fear, or emotional wounds. It also helps to bring back memories or past experiences so the participant could deal with the adverse and lasting effects they might have had on him/her.

When working on the clay individuals are immersed in the activity, pouring their experiences of pain, sorrow, anger and abuse without having to utter a word. This is phenomenally relieving for those with speech inhibition and children who are too young to express emotion.

Clay therapy helps solve the most complicated problems of the individual which are far beyond his consciousness.

Clay Therapy Sessions

There are various settings for clay therapy sessions. Some are carried out in tandem with the chanting of a certain mantras and deep breathing. There might even be shoulder messages, some yoga practices, the discerning of pressure points etc.

Sometimes, members of the group unite in joining hands to embrace the positive spirit that emerges from this unique practice.

The environment is conducive to the expression of oneself. The individual is allowed to be him/herself and declare his identity. The medium allows participants to confront their innermost issues and deal with them. This eventually leads to inner growth and tranquility.

Final Words

There is a point where we would wish for nothing more than to mend some of the fragments in our life. Despair, tragedy, monotony, illness, etc. are what life inevitably entails. Simultaneously, however, joy, hope, love, success, change for the good are also part of life. Unequivocally, some of the positive facets of life may be hard to obtain following some traumatic events. But, hey, you're not alone— in fact, you are far from being alone, as there are thousands and millions of children, adults, senior citizens around the world experiencing the same or even worse.

This book is for people who are struggling with depression, anxiety, stress, dementia, and other mental health issues. It is also for people who want to stretch a hand to those who are experiencing one or more of the issues mentioned above.

Expressive therapy will help you or those around you to overcome some of the challenges and setbacks that standard therapy can't present. It's proven to be a very effectual form of medicine and it has helped several people express themselves efficiently and have risen to the point of self-discovery.

Grab this opportunity to let one of the expressive therapies change your walk of life. Consult a therapist to give you further notes on the subject if you feel it's needed.

Take good care and good luck!